Best of South Korea

Top Spots to Explore

© 2024 James Anthony Chambers. All rights reserved.
No part of this book may be reproduced, distributed, or transmitted in any form or by any means, including photocopying, recording, or other electronic or mechanical methods, without the prior written permission of the publisher, except in the case of brief quotations embodied in critical reviews and certain other noncommercial uses permitted by copyright law.
This travel guide was written with the assistance of ChatGPT, an AI language model developed by OpenAI, to provide accurate and up-to-date information. The pictures featured on the cover of this book are license-free images sourced from Canva.

Intro 6

Seoul: Dynamic Capital Delights 8

Gyeongbokgung Palace: Timeless Majesty 10

Bukchon Hanok Village: Heritage in Harmony 12

Myeongdong: Shopper's Paradise 14

N Seoul Tower: Iconic City Views 16

Insadong: Tradition Alive 18

DMZ: A Journey to the Edge 20

Jeju Island: Nature's Paradise 22

Seongsan Ilchulbong: Sunrise Summit 24

Haeundae Beach: Coastal Charm 26

Busan Gamcheon Culture Village: Colourful Escapade 28

Jagalchi Fish Market: Seafood Sensation 30

Gwangalli Beach: Twilight Serenity 32

Beomeosa Temple: Tranquil Retreat 34

Andong Hahoe Folk Village: Living Heritage 36

Daegu E-world: Thrills and Chills 38

Tongyeong Cable Car: Skyline Soar 40

Boseong Green Tea Fields: Verdant Beauty 42

Jeonju Hanok Village: Culinary Capital 44

Nami Island: Romantic Hideaway 47

Everland: Magic of Adventure 49

Lotte World: Fantasy Escapade 51

Korean Folk Village: Living History 53

Yongpyong Ski Resort: Winter Wonderland 55

Seoraksan National Park: Majestic Peaks 57

Hwaseong Fortress: Ancient Defense 60

Suwon: City of Filial Piety 62

Gyeongju: Time Capsule of Korea 64

Bulguksa Temple: Serene Splendor 66

Seokguram Grotto: Buddhist Treasure 68

Changdeokgung Palace: Secret Garden Stroll 70

Hallyu Experience: K-Pop and Beyond 72

Korean Demilitarized Zone: Border of Intrigue 75

Boseong Tea Plantations: Sip of Tranquility 77

Daejeon: Science City Marvels 79

Korean War Memorial: Tribute to Valor 81

Jinhae Cherry Blossom Festival: Pink Petal Extravaganza 83

Jjimjilbang Experience: Relaxation Ritual 85

Sokcho: Gateway to Seoraksan 88

Taebaeksan Snow Festival: Frosty Fiesta 91

Cheonggyecheon Stream: Urban Oasis 94

Jeonju Bibimbap: Culinary Heritage 97

Gyeongju Bulguksa Temple: Spiritual Haven 100

Incheon: Gateway to the World 103

Afterword 106

Intro

As you step onto the bustling streets of South Korea, you're not just entering a country; you're embarking on a journey into a world where tradition dances with modernity, where history whispers its tales amidst skyscrapers, and where nature's beauty unfolds in serene landscapes. This enchanting land, nestled on the eastern edge of Asia, holds a treasure trove of experiences waiting to be discovered.

Picture yourself wandering through the vibrant streets of Seoul, the beating heart of South Korea. Here, amidst the neon lights and bustling markets, ancient palaces stand as silent witnesses to the country's rich heritage. Gyeongbokgung Palace, with its majestic gates and ornate halls, invites you to step back in time and immerse yourself in the grandeur of Korea's royal past.

But South Korea is not just about its capital; venture further, and you'll find yourself on the enchanting island of Jeju, where emerald waters lap against dramatic cliffs, and volcanic landscapes tell tales of ancient eruptions. Explore the labyrinthine caves of Manjanggul or marvel at the sunrise from the summit of Seongsan Ilchulbong, and you'll understand why Jeju is often called the "Island of the Gods."

For those seeking a taste of adventure, the rugged peaks of Seoraksan National Park beckon. Here, amidst towering granite cliffs and cascading waterfalls, you can hike through pristine forests and breathe in the crisp mountain air. And when winter blankets the landscape in snow, Yongpyong Ski Resort comes alive, offering exhilarating slopes and cozy apres-ski retreats.

But South Korea is not just about nature and history; it's also a land of vibrant culture and modern innovation. Lose yourself in the pulsating energy of Seoul's nightlife, where K-pop beats pulse through crowded clubs, or indulge in the latest fashion trends in the trendy boutiques of Gangnam.

As you turn the pages of this guide, allow yourself to be transported to the myriad wonders of South Korea. From the bustling streets of Seoul to the tranquil temples of Gyeongju, each chapter invites you to uncover a new facet of this captivating country. So, pack your bags, and get ready to embark on the adventure of a lifetime.

Seoul: Dynamic Capital Delights

In the heart of South Korea lies a city that pulses with life, a metropolis where ancient traditions blend seamlessly with modern innovation – Seoul, the dynamic capital of the nation. As you step into this vibrant urban landscape, you'll find yourself immersed in a whirlwind of sights, sounds, and experiences that captivate the senses and stir the soul.

Seoul is a city of contrasts, where towering skyscrapers cast shadows over ancient palaces, and bustling markets sit alongside serene temples. At its core lies a rich tapestry of history, shaped by centuries of royal dynasties and turbulent upheavals. Gyeongbokgung Palace, with its majestic gates and sweeping courtyards, stands as a testament to the glory of Korea's Joseon Dynasty, while Changdeokgung Palace offers a glimpse into the secluded world of the royal family with its secret garden retreats.

But Seoul is not just a city frozen in time; it is a living, breathing entity that evolves with each passing moment. Nowhere is this more evident than in the bustling streets of Myeongdong, where neon signs compete for attention amidst a sea of shoppers and street food vendors tempt passersby with their tantalising aromas. Here, amidst the chaos, you'll discover the pulse of modern Seoul – a vibrant energy that propels the city forward into the future.

Yet, amidst the hustle and bustle of urban life, Seoul remains a city deeply rooted in tradition and spirituality. In the quiet corners of Bukchon Hanok Village, ancient wooden houses line narrow alleyways, offering a glimpse into Korea's past. Here, you can wander the labyrinthine streets, lose yourself in the beauty of traditional architecture, and experience the timeless elegance of hanbok-clad locals.

As night falls, Seoul transforms into a playground of lights and laughter, where the city's vibrant nightlife comes alive. From the trendy clubs of Gangnam to the hidden speakeasies of Itaewon, there's no shortage of excitement to be found in the city after dark. And for those seeking a taste of the avant-garde, the Dongdaemun Design Plaza stands as a beacon of creativity, showcasing the cutting-edge designs of Korea's brightest talents.

Seoul is a city that defies expectations, a place where the past and present collide in a kaleidoscope of culture and creativity. Whether you're exploring ancient palaces or dancing the night away in a trendy club, one thing is certain – in Seoul, the possibilities are endless, and the adventure never ends.

Gyeongbokgung Palace: Timeless Majesty

In the heart of Seoul, amidst the modern skyline and bustling streets, lies a majestic reminder of Korea's royal heritage – Gyeongbokgung Palace. Steeped in history and surrounded by myth, this sprawling complex stands as a testament to the grandeur of the Joseon Dynasty, a time when emperors ruled with absolute authority and the arts flourished in the shadow of towering palace walls.

As you approach the palace gates, you can't help but feel a sense of awe at the sheer scale and beauty of the architecture before you. Built in 1395 by King Taejo, the founder of the Joseon Dynasty, Gyeongbokgung served as the main royal residence for over two centuries, housing the throne room, government offices, and living quarters for the royal family.

But Gyeongbokgung is more than just a collection of buildings; it's a living museum, a window into Korea's past. As you step through the gates and into the inner courtyard, you'll find yourself transported back in time to an era of courtly intrigue and royal splendour. The main hall, Geunjeongjeon, with its intricate wooden carvings and towering columns, once played host to lavish state ceremonies and royal audiences, while the nearby Gyeonghoeru Pavilion served as the backdrop for extravagant banquets and celebrations.

Yet, amidst the opulence of the palace grounds, there are reminders of the challenges faced by Korea's rulers. The nearby National Folk Museum offers a glimpse into the daily lives of ordinary Koreans, showcasing traditional crafts, rituals, and customs that have been passed down through generations. And just beyond the palace walls lies the imposing figure of Gwanghwamun Gate, a symbol of Korea's resilience in the face of adversity.

But perhaps the most enchanting aspect of Gyeongbokgung Palace is its ability to transcend time, to bridge the gap between past and present. As you wander the tranquil gardens and admire the intricate details of the architecture, you can't help but feel a sense of connection to the generations of Koreans who walked these same paths before you. In a city that's constantly evolving, Gyeongbokgung Palace stands as a timeless reminder of Korea's rich cultural heritage – a treasure to be cherished and preserved for generations to come.

Bukchon Hanok Village: Heritage in Harmony

Nestled amidst the bustling streets of modern Seoul, there lies a hidden gem that offers a glimpse into Korea's storied past – Bukchon Hanok Village. Tucked away between the towering skyscrapers and bustling markets, this charming neighbourhood is a living testament to Korea's traditional architecture and way of life, where ancient hanok houses stand in harmony with the urban landscape.

As you step into Bukchon Hanok Village, you'll feel as though you've entered a time warp, transported back to a bygone era of wooden houses and tiled roofs. The narrow alleyways wind their way through the neighbourhood, revealing hidden courtyards and secret gardens, each one more enchanting than the last.

But Bukchon Hanok Village is more than just a collection of old houses; it's a living, breathing community where tradition and modernity coexist in perfect harmony. Here, amidst the quiet streets and tiled rooftops, you'll find local residents going about their daily lives, tending to gardens, and carrying on centuries-old traditions.

Wandering through the village, you'll come across a wealth of cultural treasures, from traditional tea houses and artisan workshops to galleries showcasing the works of local artists. And at the heart of it all lies the Bukchon Traditional Culture Center, where visitors can learn about the history and heritage of the neighbourhood through interactive exhibits and guided tours.

But perhaps the most enchanting aspect of Bukchon Hanok Village is its ability to transport you back in time while still being firmly rooted in the present. As you explore the narrow alleyways and soak in the sights and sounds of this historic neighbourhood, you'll come to appreciate the delicate balance between preservation and progress that defines modern Seoul.

In a city that's constantly evolving, Bukchon Hanok Village stands as a timeless reminder of Korea's rich cultural heritage – a place where the past meets the present in perfect harmony, and where the spirit of tradition lives on in every wooden beam and tiled roof.

Myeongdong: Shopper's Paradise

In the heart of Seoul, where the pulse of the city beats strongest, lies a district that beckons to shoppers with promises of endless delights and treasures waiting to be discovered – Myeongdong. As you step into this bustling neighbourhood, you'll find yourself swept up in a whirlwind of sights, sounds, and scents, as vendors call out to passersby and neon signs beckon from every corner.

Myeongdong is a shopper's paradise, a labyrinth of streets and alleys lined with an eclectic mix of boutiques, department stores, and street markets. Here, amidst the chaos of urban life, you'll find everything your heart desires, from high-end fashion brands to quirky souvenir shops selling the latest K-pop merchandise.

But Myeongdong is more than just a place to shop; it's a sensory experience unlike any other. As you navigate the crowded streets, your senses will be assaulted by the tantalising aroma of street food stalls offering everything from spicy tteokbokki to sweet and savory hotteok. And as you browse the stalls and haggle with vendors, you'll find yourself swept up in the energy and excitement of the bustling marketplace.

Yet, amidst the chaos, there are moments of serenity to be found. Hidden amidst the maze of shops and stalls are quiet alleyways lined with charming cafes and traditional tea houses, where you can escape the hustle and bustle of the main thoroughfares and unwind with a cup of freshly brewed green tea.

But perhaps the most enchanting aspect of Myeongdong is its ability to cater to every taste and budget. Whether you're a fashionista hunting for the latest trends or a bargain hunter in search of hidden gems, you'll find something to suit your style and budget in this vibrant district.

In a city that's constantly evolving, Myeongdong remains a beacon of commerce and culture, a place where tradition meets modernity and shoppers of all ages and backgrounds come together to indulge in the timeless pleasure of retail therapy. So, pack your bags and prepare to lose yourself in the vibrant streets of Myeongdong – for in this shopper's paradise, the possibilities are endless, and the adventure never ends.

N Seoul Tower: Iconic City Views

Perched atop Namsan Mountain, overlooking the sprawling expanse of Seoul, stands an iconic landmark that has come to symbolize the city's vibrant spirit and unyielding ambition – N Seoul Tower. Rising majestically above the urban skyline, this towering structure offers visitors an unparalleled opportunity to witness Seoul in all its glory, from the glittering lights of the city below to the distant mountains that frame the horizon.

As you ascend the tower's sleek exterior in the glass-walled elevator, anticipation builds with each passing floor. And when you finally step out onto the observation deck, you're greeted by a breathtaking panorama that stretches as far as the eye can see. From this vantage point, you can take in the full sweep of Seoul's skyline, with its towering skyscrapers, bustling streets, and winding rivers weaving their way through the urban landscape.

But N Seoul Tower offers more than just spectacular views; it's also a hub of activity and excitement, where visitors can immerse themselves in a world of entertainment and culture. Step inside the tower, and you'll find an array of attractions waiting to be explored, from interactive exhibitions showcasing the city's history and culture to a revolving restaurant where you can dine in style while taking in the ever-changing views.

For the adventurous at heart, there's even the option to embark on a thrilling skywalk around the tower's exterior, allowing you to experience the city from a whole new perspective. And as night falls and the city lights up below, N Seoul Tower takes on a magical quality, casting its warm glow over the city and offering a romantic backdrop for couples seeking a memorable evening out.

But perhaps the most enchanting aspect of N Seoul Tower is its ability to bring people together, to serve as a beacon of hope and unity in a city that's constantly evolving. Whether you're a visitor marvelling at the sights or a local returning to this beloved landmark time and time again, N Seoul Tower holds a special place in the hearts of all who call Seoul home.

So, whether you're seeking panoramic views, cultural enrichment, or simply a moment of quiet contemplation amidst the hustle and bustle of urban life, N Seoul Tower offers something for everyone. As you stand atop this iconic landmark, gazing out over the city below, you'll come to understand why N Seoul Tower is more than just a tourist attraction – it's a symbol of Seoul's enduring spirit and unwavering determination to reach ever greater heights.

Insadong: Tradition Alive

Nestled amidst the bustling streets of modern Seoul lies a neighbourhood that feels like a step back in time – Insadong. Here, amidst the sleek glass facades and neon signs of the city, you'll find yourself transported to a world where tradition is not just preserved but celebrated, where ancient customs and crafts continue to thrive in the heart of the urban landscape.

As you wander the narrow alleyways of Insadong, you'll be greeted by a kaleidoscope of sights, sounds, and smells that tantalise the senses and ignite the imagination. Traditional hanok houses line the streets, their wooden facades adorned with intricate carvings and colourful paintwork, while the air is filled with the scent of incense and freshly brewed tea.

But Insadong is more than just a museum of the past; it's a living, breathing neighbourhood where tradition is woven into the fabric of everyday life. Here, amidst the quaint tea houses and artisan workshops, you'll find locals going about their daily routines, practicing age-old crafts and preserving the customs of their ancestors.

One of the highlights of Insadong is its vibrant arts scene, with galleries showcasing the works of both established and up-and-coming artists. From traditional ink paintings to contemporary sculptures, there's something to suit every taste and style, making Insadong a haven for art lovers from around the world.

But perhaps the most enchanting aspect of Insadong is its bustling market, where vendors peddle a dizzying array of traditional goods and handicrafts. From delicate ceramics and intricately woven textiles to handmade jewellery and wooden masks, there's no shortage of treasures to be found amidst the crowded stalls and bustling crowds.

As you explore Insadong, you'll come to appreciate the delicate balance between past and present that defines modern Seoul. In a city that's constantly evolving, Insadong stands as a timeless reminder of Korea's rich cultural heritage – a place where tradition is not just preserved but cherished, and where the spirit of the past lives on in every stone and brushstroke. So, whether you're a history buff, an art aficionado, or simply curious to experience the magic of old-world Seoul, Insadong offers an unforgettable journey back in time.

DMZ: A Journey to the Edge

Nestled along the border between North and South Korea lies a stretch of land that has come to symbolize the stark divide between two nations – the Demilitarized Zone, or DMZ. This narrow strip of land, stretching for 250 kilometers across the Korean Peninsula, serves as a poignant reminder of the unresolved tensions that continue to simmer beneath the surface of the Korean conflict.

As you embark on a journey to the DMZ, you'll find yourself stepping into a world unlike any other – a world where barbed wire fences and military checkpoints stand as silent sentinels along the border, and where the echoes of history reverberate through the tranquil landscape.

The DMZ is a place of contradictions, where the beauty of the natural surroundings clashes with the harsh realities of geopolitics. Here, amidst lush forests and rolling hills, you'll encounter a landscape that belies the tension and uncertainty that hangs in the air.

One of the highlights of any visit to the DMZ is a tour of the Joint Security Area, or JSA, where visitors can catch a glimpse of North Korea from the safety of the South Korean side. Standing just meters away from the border, you'll find yourself face to face with North Korean soldiers, their stoic expressions a reminder of the divide that separates their country from the outside world.

But the DMZ is not just a place of confrontation and conflict; it's also a testament to the resilience of the human spirit. Amidst the military installations and watchtowers, you'll find signs of life – from the thriving ecosystems that have reclaimed the land to the small communities of farmers who call the DMZ home.

As you journey through the DMZ, you'll come to appreciate the complexity of the Korean conflict and the profound impact it has had on the lives of millions of people. Whether you're standing on the edge of the border, peering into the forbidden territory of North Korea, or walking through the tunnels dug by North Korean soldiers in a bid to infiltrate the South, each step brings you closer to understanding the fragile balance of power that defines the Korean Peninsula.

In a world that's often defined by borders and divisions, the DMZ serves as a powerful reminder of the need for dialogue and diplomacy in resolving conflicts. And as you stand on the edge of this geopolitical fault line, you'll come to appreciate the importance of seeking peace and understanding in a world that's too often torn apart by division and mistrust.

Jeju Island: Nature's Paradise

Off the southern coast of the Korean Peninsula lies a jewel of the East Sea, a place where emerald waters lap against pristine shores and volcanic landscapes tell tales of ancient eruptions – Jeju Island. Renowned for its breathtaking natural beauty and unique geological features, Jeju has earned its reputation as "Nature's Paradise," drawing visitors from far and wide to experience its wonders firsthand.

As you arrive on the island, you'll be greeted by a sense of tranquillity that permeates the air, a feeling of being embraced by nature's embrace. The island's lush landscapes, dotted with forests, waterfalls, and rolling hills, offer a welcome respite from the hustle and bustle of city life, inviting you to slow down and reconnect with the natural world.

One of the highlights of any visit to Jeju is a journey to the summit of Hallasan, the island's iconic volcano and the highest peak in South Korea. As you trek through the UNESCO-listed Hallasan National Park, you'll find yourself surrounded by a kaleidoscope of flora and fauna, from rare orchids and azaleas to native bird species that call the mountain home.

But Jeju's natural wonders extend far beyond its volcanic landscapes. Along the island's rugged coastline, you'll discover hidden coves and secluded beaches where crystal-clear waters beckon swimmers and sunbathers alike. Whether you're exploring the dramatic cliffs of Seongsan Ilchulbong or lounging on the sandy shores of Hyeopjae Beach, there's no shortage of idyllic spots to soak up the sun and sea.

For those seeking a taste of adventure, Jeju offers a wealth of outdoor activities to suit every interest and skill level. From hiking and horseback riding to diving and snorkelling, there's something for everyone to enjoy amidst the island's natural playground.

But perhaps the most enchanting aspect of Jeju is its sense of serenity, its ability to inspire awe and wonder in those who traverse its landscapes. Whether you're wandering through the mystical lava tubes of Manjanggul or admiring the sunrise from the peak of Seongsan Ilchulbong, each moment spent on Jeju feels like a gift from nature itself.

In a world that's increasingly dominated by concrete jungles and artificial landscapes, Jeju Island stands as a testament to the power and beauty of the natural world. So, pack your bags and prepare to embark on an unforgettable journey to "Nature's Paradise" – for on Jeju Island, the wonders of the natural world await at every turn.

Seongsan Ilchulbong: Sunrise Summit

Perched on the eastern edge of Jeju Island, overlooking the sparkling waters of the East Sea, stands a natural wonder that captivates the hearts of all who behold it – Seongsan Ilchulbong, also known as Sunrise Peak. Rising dramatically from the sea, this majestic volcanic crater is a sight to behold, its jagged cliffs and verdant slopes bathed in the golden light of dawn.

For generations, Seongsan Ilchulbong has been revered as a sacred site, a place where locals gather to witness the breathtaking spectacle of the sunrise. As the first light of day breaks over the horizon, casting a warm glow across the landscape, visitors gather atop the peak to marvel at the beauty of nature's daily miracle.

But Seongsan Ilchulbong is more than just a vantage point for sunrise seekers; it's also a paradise for outdoor enthusiasts and nature lovers alike. As you ascend the steep trail that winds its way to the summit, you'll find yourself surrounded by a tapestry of vibrant flora and fauna, from rare orchids and wildflowers to native bird species that call the crater home.

At the summit, you'll be rewarded with panoramic views that stretch as far as the eye can see, encompassing the rugged coastline of Jeju Island and the distant peaks of Hallasan. Below, the turquoise waters of the sea sparkle in the morning light, while fishing boats ply their trade along the rocky shores.

For the adventurous at heart, there's even the option to hike along the crater rim, offering a thrilling perspective of Seongsan Ilchulbong's sheer cliffs and volcanic formations. And as you explore the crater's interior, you'll discover hidden caves and rock formations that speak to the island's geological history.

But perhaps the most magical moment comes as the sun breaks free from the horizon, casting its warm rays across the landscape and painting the sky in a palette of fiery hues. As you watch in awe, surrounded by fellow travellers from around the world, you'll come to understand why Seongsan Ilchulbong is considered one of Jeju's most iconic landmarks – a place where the beauty of nature takes center stage and the wonder of the world unfolds before your eyes.

Haeundae Beach: Coastal Charm

Perched on the southeastern tip of the Korean Peninsula, where the azure waters of the East Sea meet the golden sands of the shore, lies a coastal gem that beckons travellers from far and wide – Haeundae Beach. Renowned for its pristine beauty and vibrant atmosphere, Haeundae is a destination that captures the essence of seaside charm, offering visitors an escape from the hustle and bustle of urban life.

As you approach Haeundae Beach, you'll be greeted by the gentle sound of waves lapping against the shore and the salty tang of sea air that fills your lungs. The sweeping curve of the coastline stretches out before you, lined with palm trees and bustling with activity, as locals and tourists alike flock to the beach to soak up the sun and surf.

But Haeundae is more than just a place to sunbathe and swim; it's a hub of seaside entertainment and leisure, where visitors can indulge in a wealth of activities to suit every interest and inclination. From water sports like jet skiing and parasailing to beach volleyball and sandcastle building, there's something for everyone to enjoy amidst the sun-drenched shores.

For those seeking a taste of culture and history, Haeundae offers a wealth of attractions to explore. Just steps from the beach lies the Dongbaekseom Island, home to the APEC Nurimaru House and the picturesque Dongbaek Park, where visitors can stroll amidst lush gardens and scenic walking trails while taking in panoramic views of the coastline.

And when hunger strikes, Haeundae's vibrant food scene has you covered, with a plethora of beachfront cafes, seafood restaurants, and street food stalls offering a taste of local delicacies. From freshly caught fish and seafood platters to spicy tteokbokki and crispy fried chicken, there's no shortage of culinary delights to tempt your taste buds.

But perhaps the most enchanting aspect of Haeundae Beach is its sense of community and camaraderie, where visitors from all walks of life come together to share in the simple pleasures of seaside living. Whether you're lounging on the sand with a good book, taking a leisurely stroll along the boardwalk, or simply soaking in the sights and sounds of the beach, Haeundae offers a slice of coastal paradise that's sure to leave a lasting impression.

Busan Gamcheon Culture Village: Colourful Escapade

Nestled amidst the rolling hills of Busan, overlooking the sparkling waters of the East Sea, lies a neighbourhood that bursts with vibrant hues and whimsical charm – Gamcheon Culture Village. Perched on the slopes of a hillside, this once-sleepy fishing village has undergone a remarkable transformation, emerging as a kaleidoscope of colours and creativity that captures the imagination of all who visit.

As you make your way through the narrow alleyways of Gamcheon Culture Village, you'll find yourself surrounded by a riot of colours – from pastel-hued houses and brightly painted murals to whimsical sculptures and quirky installations that dot the landscape. Each corner reveals a new surprise, a hidden gem waiting to be discovered amidst the maze of winding streets and staircases.

But Gamcheon Culture Village is more than just a feast for the eyes; it's also a living, breathing community where art and culture thrive. Here, amidst the vibrant street art and quirky cafes, you'll find local artists and artisans at work, their creativity on full display as they transform the village into a living canvas.

One of the highlights of any visit to Gamcheon Culture Village is the chance to interact with the locals and learn about the history and heritage of the neighbourhood. From guided walking tours led by knowledgeable guides to hands-on workshops and cultural performances, there's no shortage of opportunities to immerse yourself in the rich tapestry of Gamcheon's past and present.

For those seeking panoramic views of the village and its surroundings, a trek to the hilltop observatory offers a breathtaking perspective of Gamcheon's colourful rooftops and winding streets. From this vantage point, you can marvel at the beauty of the village below and appreciate the ingenuity of its inhabitants in transforming a humble fishing village into a cultural oasis.

But perhaps the most enchanting aspect of Gamcheon Culture Village is its sense of community and camaraderie, where visitors from all walks of life come together to celebrate art, culture, and creativity. Whether you're exploring the maze-like streets, admiring the vibrant murals, or simply soaking in the atmosphere of this whimsical neighbourhood, Gamcheon offers a colourful escapade that's sure to leave a lasting impression.

Jagalchi Fish Market: Seafood Sensation

Nestled on the shores of Busan, where the salty tang of sea air mingles with the hustle and bustle of daily life, lies a culinary paradise that promises to tantalise the taste buds and delight the senses – Jagalchi Fish Market. Renowned as one of Korea's largest seafood markets, Jagalchi is a vibrant hub of activity where locals and tourists alike come together to sample the freshest catches of the day and immerse themselves in the rich maritime culture of Busan.

As you enter Jagalchi Fish Market, you'll be greeted by a symphony of sights, sounds, and smells that beckon you deeper into its labyrinthine corridors. Rows of stalls line the narrow aisles, their tables overflowing with an astonishing array of seafood – from plump prawns and succulent crabs to gleaming fish and exotic shellfish.

But Jagalchi is more than just a market; it's a sensory experience unlike any other, where the sights and sounds of the sea come alive in a whirlwind of activity. Fishmongers call out to passersby, haggling over prices and extolling the virtues of their wares, while the clatter of knives and the sizzle of grills fill the air with a symphony of culinary delights.

For those with an adventurous palate, Jagalchi offers the opportunity to sample some of Korea's most beloved seafood dishes, prepared fresh to order by expert chefs right before your eyes. From spicy seafood stew and grilled octopus to raw fish sashimi and crispy tempura, there's something to suit every taste and craving amidst the market's bustling food stalls.

But perhaps the most enchanting aspect of Jagalchi Fish Market is its sense of tradition and heritage, rooted in centuries of maritime culture and coastal living. As you wander the aisles and interact with the vendors, you'll come to appreciate the deep connection that Busan's residents have to the sea – a connection that's reflected in every gleaming fish and shimmering shellfish on display.

Whether you're a seafood aficionado eager to sample the freshest catches of the day or a curious traveller keen to immerse yourself in the vibrant culinary scene of Busan, Jagalchi Fish Market promises an unforgettable experience that's sure to leave you craving more. So, pack your appetite and prepare to embark on a seafood sensation that's as delicious as it is delightful.

Gwangalli Beach: Twilight Serenity

As the sun dips below the horizon, casting a warm glow across the tranquil waters of the Gwangalli Beach, a sense of serenity settles over the bustling city of Busan. Nestled between towering skyscrapers and rolling hills, Gwangalli Beach is a haven of calm amidst the urban chaos, offering visitors a chance to unwind and reconnect with nature against the backdrop of the city's glittering skyline.

As evening falls, the beach comes alive with the soft glow of twinkling lights, casting a magical spell over the shoreline. Couples stroll hand in hand along the sandy promenade, while families gather to enjoy picnics and games on the beach. The gentle sound of waves lapping against the shore provides a soothing soundtrack to the evening's activities, as visitors pause to take in the beauty of the twilight hour.

But Gwangalli Beach is not just a place to relax and unwind; it's also a hub of activity and entertainment, with a vibrant nightlife scene that draws locals and tourists alike. From seaside cafes and restaurants serving up fresh seafood delicacies to lively bars and clubs pulsating with music and energy, there's something for everyone to enjoy amidst the beachfront buzz.

One of the highlights of any visit to Gwangalli Beach is the chance to witness the spectacular Gwangan Bridge illuminated against the night sky. Stretching gracefully across the bay, this iconic bridge is a sight to behold, its arches bathed in a rainbow of colours that dance and shimmer in the darkness. As night falls, visitors gather along the beachfront to watch in awe as the bridge comes alive with light, casting a magical glow over the waters below.

For those seeking a taste of adventure, Gwangalli Beach offers a range of water sports and activities to suit every interest and skill level. From kayaking and paddleboarding to jet skiing and parasailing, there's no shortage of ways to get out on the water and experience the beauty of the beach from a whole new perspective.

But perhaps the most enchanting aspect of Gwangalli Beach is its ability to capture the essence of twilight serenity – a fleeting moment of peace and tranquillity that washes over the beach like a gentle wave. Whether you're watching the sun set behind the distant mountains or simply soaking in the atmosphere of the beach at dusk, Gwangalli offers a magical escape from the hustle and bustle of everyday life, inviting you to pause, reflect, and embrace the beauty of the moment.

Beomeosa Temple: Tranquil Retreat

Nestled amidst the lush forests of Geumjeongsan Mountain, just a short distance from the bustling city of Busan, lies a sanctuary of peace and tranquillity – Beomeosa Temple. For over a thousand years, this ancient temple has served as a spiritual retreat for monks and visitors alike, offering a respite from the chaos of everyday life and a chance to reconnect with nature and the divine.

As you approach Beomeosa Temple, the scent of incense fills the air, mingling with the sound of chanting monks and the gentle rustle of leaves in the breeze. The temple's ornate gate, known as the Iljumun Gate, stands as a guardian at the entrance, its intricate carvings and vibrant colours welcoming visitors to this sacred space.

Stepping through the gate, you'll find yourself in a world of serenity and beauty, where ancient pagodas and prayer halls nestle amidst towering pine trees and bubbling streams. The temple's main hall, known as the Daeungjeon Hall, is a masterpiece of traditional Korean architecture, its elegant lines and graceful curves reflecting the harmony of the natural world.

But Beomeosa Temple is more than just a place of worship; it's also a living testament to Korea's rich cultural heritage and Buddhist traditions. As you explore the temple grounds, you'll encounter a wealth of historical and cultural treasures, from ancient stone carvings and wooden sculptures to priceless relics and sacred scriptures.

For those seeking a deeper spiritual experience, Beomeosa offers the opportunity to participate in traditional Buddhist practices such as meditation, chanting, and temple stay programs. Whether you're a seasoned practitioner or a curious beginner, the temple's serene surroundings provide the perfect backdrop for introspection and self-discovery.

But perhaps the most enchanting aspect of Beomeosa Temple is its ability to transport visitors to a state of inner peace and tranquillity, where the stresses of modern life melt away and a sense of harmony prevails. Whether you're sitting in quiet contemplation by a mountain stream or joining in the rhythmic chants of the monks, Beomeosa offers a glimpse into a world of timeless wisdom and spiritual renewal.

As you bid farewell to Beomeosa Temple and return to the hustle and bustle of everyday life, you'll carry with you the memory of this tranquil retreat – a sanctuary of peace and beauty nestled amidst the mountains of Busan, where the soul finds solace and the spirit finds renewal.

Andong Hahoe Folk Village: Living Heritage

Nestled along the banks of the Nakdong River in the heart of South Korea's Gyeongsangbuk-do province lies a living testament to the country's rich cultural heritage – Andong Hahoe Folk Village. Stepping into this historic village feels like stepping back in time, as traditional hanok houses and thatched-roof cottages dot the landscape, preserving the customs and way of life of generations past.

As you wander the cobbled streets of Hahoe Folk Village, you'll find yourself surrounded by a world of ancient traditions and timeless beauty. The village's well-preserved architecture and historic landmarks offer a glimpse into Korea's agrarian past, with wooden houses and tiled roofs that harken back to a simpler time.

But Hahoe Folk Village is more than just a museum; it's a living, breathing community where descendants of the village's founding families still reside, carrying on the traditions and customs of their ancestors. As you explore the village, you may encounter locals going about their daily routines – tending to crops in the fields, weaving traditional textiles, or practicing age-old crafts such as pottery and calligraphy.

One of the highlights of any visit to Hahoe Folk Village is the chance to experience traditional Korean culture firsthand through a range of cultural activities and performances. From mask dances and folk music concerts to hands-on workshops in traditional crafts, there's no shortage of ways to immerse yourself in the rich cultural heritage of the village.

For those interested in delving deeper into the history of Hahoe, a visit to the Hahoe Folk Museum offers a fascinating glimpse into the village's past, with exhibits showcasing artifacts and photographs that tell the story of its evolution over the centuries. And for those seeking a moment of tranquillity amidst the hustle and bustle of village life, the picturesque Buyongdae Cliff offers panoramic views of the surrounding countryside, providing the perfect spot for reflection and contemplation.

But perhaps the most enchanting aspect of Hahoe Folk Village is its sense of community and camaraderie, where visitors are welcomed with open arms and invited to share in the timeless traditions of the village. Whether you're participating in a traditional ceremony or simply strolling through the tranquil streets, Hahoe offers a glimpse into a world where the past and present coexist in perfect harmony – a living heritage that continues to inspire and captivate all who visit.

Daegu E-world: Thrills and Chills

Nestled amidst the vibrant cityscape of Daegu lies a world of excitement and adventure waiting to be discovered – E-world. This thrilling amusement park offers a kaleidoscope of attractions, from pulse-pounding rides and exhilarating roller coasters to family-friendly entertainment and dazzling nighttime spectacles.

As you approach E-world, you'll be greeted by the sight of towering Ferris wheels and twisting roller coasters that pierce the sky, their neon lights casting a mesmerising glow over the city below. The air is alive with the sounds of laughter and excitement as visitors of all ages flock to experience the thrills and chills that await within.

One of the highlights of E-world is its impressive lineup of rides and attractions, catering to adrenaline junkies and thrill-seekers alike. From heart-stopping drops and gravity-defying loops to gentle spins and interactive experiences, there's something for everyone to enjoy amidst the park's sprawling grounds.

For those seeking a taste of nostalgia, E-world offers a range of classic amusement park attractions, from traditional carousel rides and bumper cars to carnival games and funhouses.

And for the little ones, a dedicated children's area provides a safe and playful space where they can let their imaginations run wild.

But E-world is more than just an amusement park; it's also a hub of entertainment and excitement that extends into the evening hours. As night falls, the park comes alive with dazzling light shows and fireworks displays, illuminating the sky in a riot of colour and sound that's sure to leave a lasting impression.

For those looking to take a break from the thrills and chills, E-world also offers a range of dining and shopping options to suit every taste and budget. From gourmet restaurants and trendy cafes to souvenir shops and boutiques, there's plenty to see, do, and taste amidst the hustle and bustle of the park.

But perhaps the most enchanting aspect of E-world is its ability to transport visitors to a world of pure joy and excitement, where the worries of everyday life melt away and the spirit of adventure reigns supreme. Whether you're hurtling through the air on a roller coaster, enjoying a leisurely stroll through the park, or simply soaking in the atmosphere of this vibrant entertainment hub, E-world promises an unforgettable experience that's sure to thrill and delight all who visit.

Tongyeong Cable Car: Skyline Soar

Perched on the southern coast of South Korea, where the emerald waters of the East Sea meet the rugged cliffs of the coastline, lies a scenic gem waiting to be discovered – the Tongyeong Cable Car. This modern marvel of engineering offers visitors a chance to soar high above the city and take in breathtaking panoramic views of the surrounding landscape, making it a must-visit attraction for anyone exploring the beauty of Tongyeong.

As you board the cable car and begin your ascent, the hustle and bustle of the city below gradually fade away, replaced by a sense of tranquillity and awe as you rise above the treetops and ascend towards the heavens. The gentle hum of the cable car's machinery is accompanied by the soft rustle of leaves and the occasional chirp of birds, creating a serene atmosphere that's perfect for relaxation and reflection.

As you reach the summit, you'll be greeted by a vista that stretches as far as the eye can see – from the shimmering waters of Tongyeong Harbour to the distant peaks of nearby islands. The panoramic view offers a glimpse into the natural beauty of the region, with its lush forests, craggy cliffs, and sparkling seascape that stretches to the horizon.

But the Tongyeong Cable Car is more than just a scenic journey; it's also a gateway to adventure and exploration. At the summit, visitors can disembark and explore a network of hiking trails that wind through the surrounding hills and offer opportunities for outdoor recreation and wildlife spotting. Whether you're a seasoned hiker looking for a challenge or a casual stroller seeking a leisurely stroll, there's a trail to suit every level of experience and fitness.

For those looking to learn more about the natural and cultural history of the area, the Tongyeong Cable Car also offers access to a range of visitor facilities, including an observation deck, souvenir shop, and cafe. Here, visitors can enjoy refreshments while taking in the stunning views or browse through a selection of locally made crafts and gifts to commemorate their visit.

But perhaps the most enchanting aspect of the Tongyeong Cable Car is its ability to offer a new perspective on the beauty of Tongyeong, allowing visitors to see the city and its surroundings from a whole new angle. Whether you're soaring high above the cityscape or exploring the natural wonders of the summit, the cable car promises an unforgettable experience that's sure to leave a lasting impression on all who embark on this sky-high adventure.

Boseong Green Tea Fields: Verdant Beauty

Nestled amidst the rolling hills of Boseong County in South Korea's Jeollanam-do province lies a landscape of unparalleled beauty – the Boseong Green Tea Fields. Here, as far as the eye can see, lush rows of tea bushes blanket the hillsides, their vibrant green foliage shimmering in the sunlight like a sea of emeralds.

As you arrive at the Boseong Green Tea Fields, you'll be struck by the sheer magnitude of the landscape before you. Stretching across acres of undulating terrain, the tea fields form a patchwork of colour and texture that's both mesmerising and awe-inspiring.

But the beauty of Boseong extends far beyond its picturesque scenery; it's also a place steeped in history and tradition, with a legacy of tea cultivation that dates back centuries. As you wander through the fields, you'll learn about the meticulous process of growing and harvesting green tea, from the careful pruning of bushes to the delicate hand-picking of leaves.

For those looking to delve deeper into the world of tea culture, the Boseong Green Tea Plantation offers guided tours and educational experiences that provide insight into the art and science of tea production. Visitors can explore tea processing facilities, sample freshly brewed tea, and even try their hand at traditional tea-making techniques under the guidance of knowledgeable experts.

But perhaps the most enchanting aspect of Boseong Green Tea Fields is the sense of tranquillity and serenity that permeates the air. As you wander through the fields, surrounded by the gentle rustle of leaves and the soft murmur of streams, you'll feel a sense of calm wash over you – a feeling of connection to the natural world and the centuries-old tradition of tea cultivation.

For photographers and nature lovers, Boseong offers endless opportunities to capture the beauty of the landscape in all its glory. Whether you're admiring the sunrise over the tea-covered hills or wandering through the mist-shrouded fields at dusk, there's no shortage of breathtaking vistas to behold and memories to cherish.

But perhaps the greatest pleasure of all lies in simply immersing yourself in the verdant beauty of Boseong Green Tea Fields – to walk among the tea bushes, breathe in the fragrant aroma of freshly brewed tea, and feel a sense of wonder and appreciation for the natural world that surrounds you. In Boseong, beauty abounds at every turn, inviting you to slow down, savour the moment, and embrace the tranquillity of this green oasis amidst the hills.

Jeonju Hanok Village: Culinary Capital

Nestled in the heart of Jeonju, South Korea, lies a cultural gem that beckons travellers from far and wide – the Jeonju Hanok Village. Stepping into this historic neighbourhood feels like stepping back in time, as traditional hanok houses line the narrow cobblestone streets, preserving the rich heritage and culinary traditions of centuries past.

As you wander through the labyrinthine alleyways of Jeonju Hanok Village, you'll be greeted by the tantalising aromas of sizzling meats, bubbling stews, and freshly cooked rice cakes wafting from the numerous restaurants and street food stalls that line the streets. This culinary paradise is renowned as the birthplace of some of Korea's most beloved dishes, making it a must-visit destination for food lovers and cultural enthusiasts alike.

One of the highlights of any visit to Jeonju Hanok Village is the chance to sample the local cuisine, which boasts a rich and diverse array of flavours and ingredients. From the iconic bibimbap, a hearty rice dish topped with assorted vegetables, meat, and a spicy gochujang sauce, to the savoury jeon pancakes and crispy pajeon scallion pancakes, there's something to suit every palate and craving.

But Jeonju's culinary delights extend far beyond its signature dishes; the village is also famous for its wide variety of street food offerings, from crispy hotteok pancakes and chewy tteokbokki rice cakes to sweet hoddeok filled with brown sugar and nuts. With so many delectable treats to choose from, it's easy to spend hours wandering the streets, sampling the local fare and soaking in the vibrant atmosphere of this food lover's paradise.

For those looking to delve deeper into the culinary traditions of Jeonju, the village offers a range of culinary experiences and workshops where visitors can learn to cook traditional dishes under the guidance of expert chefs. From hands-on bibimbap-making classes to rice cake pounding demonstrations, these immersive experiences offer a unique opportunity to gain insight into the secrets of Korean cuisine.

But perhaps the most enchanting aspect of Jeonju Hanok Village is its ability to transport visitors to a world where time seems to stand still, and the traditions of the past are preserved in every stone and beam. Whether you're savouring a bowl of steaming hot soup in a centuries-old hanok restaurant or browsing the bustling markets for fresh ingredients, Jeonju offers a culinary adventure that's as rich in history as it is in flavour, inviting you to taste, explore, and savour the culinary delights of Korea's culinary capital.

Nami Island: Romantic Hideaway

Nestled amidst the azure waters of the Han River in South Korea, lies a picturesque island that captures the imagination and steals the hearts of all who visit – Nami Island. Known for its natural beauty, romantic ambience, and enchanting landscapes, Nami Island is a beloved destination for couples, nature enthusiasts, and artists seeking inspiration.

As you approach Nami Island, you'll be struck by the sight of towering trees, vibrant foliage, and winding pathways that beckon you deeper into its wooded embrace. This verdant oasis offers a welcome respite from the hustle and bustle of city life, inviting visitors to slow down, unwind, and reconnect with nature amidst its serene surroundings.

One of the highlights of any visit to Nami Island is the chance to explore its lush forests and scenic trails on foot, bicycle, or electric tram. As you wander along tree-lined pathways and meandering streams, you'll encounter a treasure trove of natural wonders, from towering sequoias and majestic gingko trees to vibrant wildflowers and exotic bird species that call the island home.

But Nami Island is more than just a natural paradise; it's also a cultural hub that celebrates art, literature, and creativity in all its forms. Throughout the island, you'll find a series of outdoor art installations, sculptures, and exhibitions that showcase the work of local and international artists, adding a touch of whimsy and wonder to the landscape.

For those seeking a taste of romance, Nami Island offers a range of activities and experiences that are sure to set hearts aflutter. Couples can stroll hand in hand along the tree-lined pathways, enjoy a leisurely picnic by the riverside, or embark on a romantic boat ride along the tranquil waters that surround the island, taking in the beauty of the scenery as they bask in each other's company.

But perhaps the most enchanting aspect of Nami Island is its ability to transport visitors to a world of pure imagination and wonder – a place where the beauty of nature and the magic of creativity come together in perfect harmony. Whether you're admiring the changing colours of the leaves in autumn, watching the cherry blossoms bloom in spring, or simply soaking in the tranquillity of the island at any time of year, Nami offers a romantic hideaway that's as enchanting as it is unforgettable.

Everland: Magic of Adventure

Nestled in the verdant hills of Yongin, just a short journey from the bustling metropolis of Seoul, lies a world of enchantment and excitement waiting to be discovered – Everland. As South Korea's largest theme park and one of the most popular attractions in the country, Everland promises a day of fun and adventure for visitors of all ages.

As you approach Everland, the first thing that strikes you is the sheer scale of the park – its sprawling grounds span over 500 acres, dotted with a myriad of attractions, rides, and entertainment options. From thrilling roller coasters and heart-pounding rides to charming themed zones and live performances, there's something for everyone to enjoy amidst the park's vibrant landscape.

One of the highlights of any visit to Everland is its diverse range of attractions, catering to adrenaline junkies and families alike. Thrill-seekers can brave the towering heights of rides like the T-Express, one of the steepest wooden roller coasters in the world, or the Thunder Falls water ride, which plunges riders down a series of exhilarating drops. Meanwhile, families can explore themed zones like Zootopia, where they can encounter exotic animals and enjoy interactive exhibits and shows.

But Everland is more than just a theme park; it's also a hub of entertainment and excitement that extends into the evening hours. As night falls, the park comes alive with dazzling light shows, fireworks displays, and parades that captivate the imagination and delight the senses. From the mesmerising Magic Time Parade to the breathtaking Moonlight Parade, there's no shortage of spectacle and wonder to behold.

For those looking to take a break from the thrills and chills, Everland also offers a range of dining and shopping options to suit every taste and budget. Whether you're craving traditional Korean cuisine, international fare, or sweet treats and snacks, you'll find plenty of options to satisfy your cravings amidst the park's bustling eateries and souvenir shops.

But perhaps the most enchanting aspect of Everland is its ability to transport visitors to a world of magic and adventure, where the worries of everyday life melt away and the spirit of fun and excitement reigns supreme. Whether you're hurtling through the air on a roller coaster, exploring themed zones and attractions, or simply soaking in the atmosphere of this vibrant entertainment hub, Everland promises an unforgettable experience that's sure to thrill and delight all who visit.

Lotte World: Fantasy Escapade

Nestled in the heart of Seoul, amidst the towering skyscrapers and bustling streets, lies a world of fantasy and adventure waiting to be explored – Lotte World. This sprawling entertainment complex is not just a theme park; it's a gateway to a realm of imagination where dreams come to life and memories are made.

As you approach Lotte World, you'll be greeted by the sight of its iconic castle, which rises majestically above the surrounding skyline, beckoning visitors to step into a world of enchantment and wonder. The park's vast grounds are divided into indoor and outdoor sections, each offering a wealth of attractions and experiences that promise to captivate the imagination and ignite the senses.

Inside Lotte World's indoor complex, visitors will find themselves transported to a world of whimsy and magic, where colourful rides, themed zones, and interactive attractions await around every corner. From thrilling roller coasters and dizzying spinning rides to gentle carousels and whimsical dark rides, there's something for everyone to enjoy amidst the park's indoor wonderland.

But Lotte World is more than just a theme park; it's also a cultural hub that celebrates the rich heritage and traditions of Korea. Throughout the park, visitors can explore themed zones that showcase the country's history, folklore, and cultural landmarks, from ancient palaces and temples to bustling marketplaces and traditional villages.

For those seeking a taste of adventure, Lotte World's outdoor section offers a range of exhilarating rides and attractions that take advantage of the park's scenic lakeside location. Visitors can brave the heights of rides like the Gyro Swing or take a leisurely boat ride around the park's picturesque lake, soaking in the beauty of the surrounding scenery as they go.

But perhaps the most enchanting aspect of Lotte World is its ability to transport visitors to a world of fantasy and escapade, where the worries of everyday life fade away and the spirit of fun and excitement reigns supreme. Whether you're exploring the indoor wonderland, riding the thrilling attractions, or simply soaking in the atmosphere of this vibrant entertainment complex, Lotte World promises an unforgettable experience that's sure to delight visitors of all ages.

Korean Folk Village: Living History

Nestled amidst the tranquil countryside of South Korea's Gyeonggi Province lies a living tableau of the country's rich cultural heritage – the Korean Folk Village. Stepping into this immersive open-air museum is like stepping back in time, as visitors are transported to a bygone era where traditional Korean life unfolds before their eyes.

As you approach the Korean Folk Village, the first thing that strikes you is its picturesque setting – rolling hills, lush forests, and meandering streams provide the perfect backdrop for this living museum of history and culture. Spread across vast acres of land, the village is home to over 260 traditional Korean houses, each meticulously restored to its original splendour and showcasing the unique architectural styles of different regions and periods.

But the Korean Folk Village is more than just a collection of buildings; it's a vibrant community where visitors can immerse themselves in the sights, sounds, and sensations of traditional Korean life. As you wander through the winding alleyways and bustling marketplaces, you'll encounter artisans practicing age-old crafts such as pottery, weaving, and calligraphy, as well as performers showcasing traditional music, dance, and martial arts.

One of the highlights of any visit to the Korean Folk Village is the chance to experience traditional Korean cuisine firsthand. The village boasts a range of restaurants and food stalls serving up authentic dishes such as bibimbap, bulgogi, and kimchi, allowing visitors to taste the flavours of Korea's culinary heritage in a picturesque setting.

But perhaps the most enchanting aspect of the Korean Folk Village is its ability to transport visitors back in time, offering a glimpse into the daily lives and customs of Korea's ancestors. From the humble farmhouses of rural peasants to the opulent residences of noble families, the village offers a snapshot of Korean society through the ages, allowing visitors to gain a deeper understanding of the country's history and culture.

Whether you're exploring the winding streets of the village, watching traditional performances, or sampling the local cuisine, the Korean Folk Village promises an unforgettable journey through the living history of South Korea – a journey that's sure to leave a lasting impression on all who visit.

Yongpyong Ski Resort: Winter Wonderland

Nestled amidst the majestic peaks of South Korea's Taebaek Mountains lies a snowy paradise that beckons winter sports enthusiasts from far and wide – Yongpyong Ski Resort. Renowned as one of the premier ski destinations in Asia, Yongpyong offers a winter wonderland of powder-white slopes, pristine pistes, and breathtaking alpine scenery that's sure to captivate the senses and ignite the spirit of adventure.

As you approach Yongpyong Ski Resort, you'll be struck by the sheer beauty of the landscape that surrounds you – towering peaks, dense forests, and glistening snowfields stretch as far as the eye can see, promising endless opportunities for outdoor recreation and exploration. The resort's extensive network of ski runs caters to skiers and snowboarders of all levels, from beginners to seasoned pros, ensuring that everyone can enjoy the thrill of gliding down the slopes amidst the stunning backdrop of the Taebaek Mountains.

But Yongpyong is more than just a ski resort; it's a winter playground that offers a wealth of activities and amenities to suit every taste and interest. In addition to its world-class ski facilities, the resort boasts a range of other winter sports and recreational activities, including snow tubing, sledding, and snowmobiling, providing endless opportunities for fun and adventure in the snow.

For those seeking a more leisurely pace, Yongpyong offers a range of amenities and services to ensure a comfortable and enjoyable stay. The resort's cosy lodges and chalets provide the perfect retreat after a day on the slopes, offering warm hospitality, hearty meals, and breathtaking views of the surrounding mountains. And for those looking to unwind and relax, the resort's spa and wellness facilities offer a range of rejuvenating treatments and therapies to soothe tired muscles and restore body and mind.

But perhaps the most enchanting aspect of Yongpyong Ski Resort is its ability to create lasting memories and forge unforgettable experiences amidst the beauty of the winter landscape. Whether you're carving turns on the slopes, exploring the surrounding wilderness, or simply savouring the tranquillity of the mountain scenery, Yongpyong promises a winter getaway that's as exhilarating as it is unforgettable – a true winter wonderland that's sure to leave a lasting impression on all who visit.

Seoraksan National Park: Majestic Peaks

Nestled in the northeastern corner of South Korea, amidst the rugged terrain of the Taebaek Mountain range, lies a natural masterpiece that captures the imagination and steals the breath away – Seoraksan National Park. Renowned for its towering peaks, lush forests, and dramatic landscapes, Seoraksan is a paradise for outdoor enthusiasts and nature lovers seeking adventure amidst the beauty of the wilderness.

As you approach Seoraksan National Park, you'll be struck by the sheer grandeur of the landscape that unfolds before you – towering granite peaks soar skyward, their rugged slopes cloaked in dense forests of pine and fir, while cascading waterfalls and crystal-clear streams carve their way through the valleys below. This pristine wilderness is home to a diverse array of flora and fauna, including rare species such as the Korean musk deer and the Asian black bear, making it a haven for wildlife enthusiasts and photographers alike.

One of the highlights of any visit to Seoraksan is the chance to explore its network of hiking trails, which wind their way through the park's rugged terrain and offer breathtaking views of the surrounding landscape. From gentle walks through verdant valleys to challenging ascents to the summit of Mount Seorak, there's a trail to suit every level of experience and fitness, providing endless opportunities for adventure and exploration.

But Seoraksan is more than just a hiking destination; it's also a cultural and spiritual hub that holds a special place in the hearts of Koreans. At the heart of the park lies Sinheungsa Temple, one of the country's oldest and most revered Buddhist temples, which has stood amidst the mountains for over a thousand years. Here, visitors can explore ancient shrines, pagodas, and prayer halls, and experience the serene beauty and tranquility of this sacred site.

For those seeking a more leisurely experience, Seoraksan National Park offers a range of other activities and attractions to enjoy. Visitors can take a scenic cable car ride to the summit of Gwongeumseong Fortress, where panoramic views of the surrounding mountains await, or relax and unwind in one of the park's hot springs, which are renowned for their therapeutic properties and natural beauty.

But perhaps the most enchanting aspect of Seoraksan National Park is its ability to inspire awe and wonder in all who visit, inviting them to immerse themselves in the majesty of nature and discover the beauty of the wilderness. Whether you're hiking through the mountains, exploring ancient temples, or simply savouring the peace and tranquility of this pristine wilderness, Seoraksan promises an unforgettable experience that's sure to leave a lasting impression on all who venture into its majestic peaks.

Hwaseong Fortress: Ancient Defense

In the heart of Suwon, South Korea, stands a testament to the ingenuity and craftsmanship of centuries past – Hwaseong Fortress. This majestic fortress, designated as a UNESCO World Heritage Site, is a living monument to Korea's rich cultural heritage and a must-visit destination for history buffs and architecture enthusiasts alike.

As you approach Hwaseong Fortress, you'll be struck by the sheer scale and grandeur of its imposing stone walls, which stretch for over five kilometers and encircle the historic city centre of Suwon. Built in the late 18th century by King Jeongjo of the Joseon Dynasty, the fortress was designed to serve as a stronghold and protect the city from foreign invasions and internal unrest.

But Hwaseong Fortress is more than just a defensive structure; it's also a masterpiece of military architecture and engineering. The fortress features an intricate network of gates, watchtowers, and bastions, each strategically positioned to provide maximum protection and visibility. Visitors can explore the various sections of the fortress, including the impressive Paldalmun Gate, which serves as the main entrance to the city, and the iconic Hwaseomun Gate, which offers panoramic views of the surrounding countryside.

One of the highlights of any visit to Hwaseong Fortress is the chance to walk along its fortified walls and experience the sense of history and heritage that permeates the air. As you stroll along the battlements, you'll be transported back in time to an era when warriors patrolled the ramparts and cannons stood ready to defend the city against enemy attack. The views from the walls are truly spectacular, offering sweeping vistas of the city below and the surrounding mountains in the distance.

But Hwaseong Fortress is more than just a historic landmark; it's also a cultural hub that celebrates the traditions and customs of Korea's past. Throughout the fortress, visitors can explore museums, exhibitions, and cultural performances that offer insight into the history and significance of this iconic site, allowing them to gain a deeper appreciation for Korea's rich cultural heritage.

Whether you're exploring the fortress walls, admiring the historic architecture, or simply soaking in the atmosphere of this ancient stronghold, Hwaseong Fortress promises an unforgettable journey through the annals of Korean history – a journey that's sure to leave a lasting impression on all who visit.

Suwon: City of Filial Piety

Nestled in the heart of Gyeonggi Province, South Korea, lies a city steeped in tradition, history, and the spirit of filial piety – Suwon. Known as the "City of Filial Piety," Suwon is a vibrant metropolis that seamlessly blends ancient traditions with modern amenities, offering visitors a glimpse into Korea's rich cultural heritage and values.

As you wander through the streets of Suwon, you'll be struck by the sense of reverence and respect that permeates the air – from the historic landmarks and temples that dot the cityscape to the bustling markets and vibrant neighbourhoods where the spirit of community thrives. Suwon's designation as the "City of Filial Piety" is a testament to its deep-rooted Confucian values, which emphasize the importance of honouring and respecting one's parents and ancestors.

One of the highlights of any visit to Suwon is the chance to explore its historic sites and cultural landmarks, which offer insight into the city's rich history and heritage. At the heart of Suwon lies Hwaseong Fortress, a UNESCO World Heritage Site and a masterpiece of military architecture and engineering. Built in the late 18th century by King Jeongjo of the Joseon Dynasty, the fortress is a symbol of Suwon's resilience and strength, and a testament to the city's commitment to preserving its cultural heritage.

But Suwon's cultural heritage extends far beyond its historic landmarks; it's also reflected in the city's vibrant arts and cultural scene. Throughout the year, Suwon plays host to a range of festivals, performances, and exhibitions that celebrate the traditions and customs of Korea's past, allowing visitors to immerse themselves in the sights, sounds, and tastes of this dynamic city.

For those seeking a taste of traditional Korean cuisine, Suwon offers a wealth of dining options that showcase the rich and diverse flavours of the region. From hearty stews and savoury pancakes to spicy kimchi and sweet treats, there's something to suit every palate and craving amidst the city's bustling eateries and street food stalls.

But perhaps the most enchanting aspect of Suwon is its ability to inspire a sense of reverence and gratitude in all who visit – whether you're exploring its historic landmarks, savouring its culinary delights, or simply soaking in the atmosphere of this vibrant city, Suwon invites you to reflect on the importance of family, tradition, and the values that bind us together as a community.

Gyeongju: Time Capsule of Korea

Nestled on the eastern coast of South Korea, amidst rolling hills and verdant countryside, lies a city that serves as a living testament to the rich tapestry of Korea's history and culture – Gyeongju. Known as the "Time Capsule of Korea," Gyeongju is a treasure trove of ancient relics, historic sites, and cultural landmarks that offer a window into the country's illustrious past.

As you wander through the streets of Gyeongju, you'll feel as though you've stepped back in time – the city's charming alleyways, traditional hanok houses, and ancient temples evoke a sense of nostalgia and wonder, transporting visitors to a bygone era when kings and warriors roamed the land and dynasties rose and fell.

One of the highlights of any visit to Gyeongju is the chance to explore its UNESCO World Heritage Sites, which include the historic Bulguksa Temple and the Seokguram Grotto. These sacred sites, built over a thousand years ago during the Silla Dynasty, are revered for their exquisite architecture, intricate carvings, and spiritual significance, and offer visitors a glimpse into Korea's religious and cultural heritage.

But Gyeongju's historical treasures extend far beyond its temples and grottoes – the city is also home to a wealth of other historic sites and cultural landmarks, including the ancient burial mounds of the Daereungwon Tomb Complex, the majestic ruins of the Gyeongju National Museum, and the picturesque Anapji Pond, which served as a royal garden during the Silla Dynasty.

For those seeking a deeper understanding of Gyeongju's rich history and culture, the city offers a range of museums, exhibitions, and cultural experiences that provide insight into the lives and customs of Korea's ancestors. Whether you're exploring the Gyeongju Historic Area, sampling traditional Korean cuisine at a local restaurant, or simply soaking in the atmosphere of this historic city, Gyeongju promises an unforgettable journey through the annals of Korean history – a journey that's sure to leave a lasting impression on all who visit.

Bulguksa Temple: Serene Splendor

Nestled amidst the tranquil hills of Gyeongju, South Korea, lies a place of serene beauty and spiritual significance – Bulguksa Temple. Regarded as one of the most important Buddhist temples in the country, Bulguksa is a masterpiece of ancient architecture and a cherished symbol of Korea's cultural heritage.

As you approach Bulguksa Temple, you'll be struck by the sense of tranquility and reverence that permeates the air – the temple's graceful pagodas, ornate halls, and verdant gardens create a peaceful oasis amidst the surrounding natural beauty. Built in the 8th century during the Silla Dynasty, Bulguksa is renowned for its exquisite craftsmanship, intricate carvings, and harmonious design, which reflect the ideals of Buddhist philosophy and aesthetics.

One of the highlights of any visit to Bulguksa Temple is the chance to explore its historic buildings and sacred relics, which offer insight into Korea's rich religious and cultural heritage. The temple complex is home to a number of notable structures, including the Daeungjeon Hall, which enshrines a golden statue of the Buddha, and the Seokgatap and Dabotap Pagodas, which are adorned with intricate carvings and inscriptions.

But Bulguksa Temple is more than just a historic landmark; it's also a place of spiritual significance and pilgrimage for Buddhists from around the world. Throughout the year, visitors can participate in rituals and ceremonies that offer insight into the practice of Korean Buddhism, from chanting and meditation sessions to prayer services and temple stays.

For those seeking a deeper understanding of Bulguksa's cultural and historical significance, the temple offers a range of exhibitions, workshops, and guided tours that provide insight into its architectural, artistic, and religious significance. Whether you're exploring the temple grounds, admiring the ancient relics, or simply soaking in the atmosphere of this sacred site, Bulguksa promises an unforgettable journey through the heart and soul of Korea's Buddhist heritage – a journey that's sure to leave a lasting impression on all who visit.

Seokguram Grotto: Buddhist Treasure

Nestled amidst the serene mountains of Gyeongju, South Korea, lies a hidden gem of Buddhist art and architecture – the Seokguram Grotto. Carved into the granite cliffs of Mount Toham, this UNESCO World Heritage Site is a marvel of ancient craftsmanship and spiritual devotion, revered as one of the finest examples of Buddhist art in the world.

As you make your way up the winding mountain path to the entrance of the grotto, you'll be struck by the sense of anticipation and reverence that fills the air. The path meanders through dense forests and lush vegetation, offering glimpses of the surrounding countryside and glimpses of the sea in the distance.

Upon reaching the entrance to the grotto, visitors are greeted by the sight of the grand stone staircase that leads to the inner sanctum. Carved into the rock face, the staircase is adorned with intricate reliefs and sculptures depicting scenes from Buddhist scripture and legend, inviting visitors to embark on a spiritual journey of enlightenment and discovery.

Stepping inside the grotto, you'll be greeted by the sight of the main chamber, which houses the iconic Seokgamoni Buddha statue. Carved from a single piece of granite, the statue is a masterpiece of ancient artistry, standing over three meters tall and exuding a sense of serenity and grace. Surrounding the Buddha are intricate carvings of Buddhist deities, disciples, and celestial beings, each rendered with meticulous detail and craftsmanship.

But the Seokguram Grotto is more than just a work of art; it's also a place of spiritual significance and pilgrimage for Buddhists from around the world. For centuries, pilgrims have made the journey to the grotto to pay their respects to the Buddha and seek blessings for health, happiness, and enlightenment.

For those seeking a deeper understanding of the grotto's cultural and historical significance, the site offers a range of exhibitions, guided tours, and educational programs that provide insight into its architectural, artistic, and religious importance. Whether you're admiring the ancient sculptures, soaking in the peaceful atmosphere, or simply contemplating the mysteries of the universe, the Seokguram Grotto promises an unforgettable journey through the heart and soul of Korea's Buddhist heritage – a journey that's sure to leave a lasting impression on all who visit.

Changdeokgung Palace: Secret Garden Stroll

Nestled amidst the bustling streets of Seoul, South Korea, lies a hidden oasis of tranquility and beauty – Changdeokgung Palace and its Secret Garden. Steeped in history and surrounded by lush greenery, this UNESCO World Heritage Site is a testament to Korea's rich cultural heritage and a must-visit destination for history enthusiasts and nature lovers alike.

As you step through the grand entrance gates of Changdeokgung Palace, you'll feel as though you've been transported back in time to the Joseon Dynasty. The palace complex, with its elegant halls, pavilions, and courtyards, is a masterpiece of traditional Korean architecture, reflecting the refined tastes and aesthetic sensibilities of Korea's royal court.

But the true highlight of any visit to Changdeokgung Palace is the chance to explore its Secret Garden, known as Huwon in Korean. Tucked away behind the palace buildings, this expansive garden is a haven of peace and serenity, offering respite from the hustle and bustle of city life.

As you wander through the winding pathways of the Secret Garden, you'll encounter a diverse array of flora and fauna, including towering trees, tranquil ponds, and vibrant flowers in bloom. The garden's carefully manicured landscapes and scenic vistas create a sense of harmony and balance, inviting visitors to pause and reflect amidst the beauty of nature.

One of the most enchanting features of the Secret Garden is its collection of pavilions, pavilions, and pavilions. These elegant structures, with their intricate wooden carvings and ornate decorations, provide the perfect backdrop for leisurely strolls and contemplative moments, offering breathtaking views of the surrounding landscape and palace buildings.

But perhaps the most magical aspect of the Secret Garden is its ability to transport visitors to another world, where time seems to stand still and the worries of everyday life fade away. Whether you're exploring the garden's hidden corners, admiring its scenic beauty, or simply soaking in the peaceful atmosphere, Changdeokgung Palace and its Secret Garden promise an unforgettable journey through the history and natural beauty of Korea – a journey that's sure to leave a lasting impression on all who visit.

Hallyu Experience: K-Pop and Beyond

Embark on a journey into the vibrant world of South Korea's entertainment industry, where the phenomenon known as "Hallyu" (the Korean Wave) has swept across the globe, captivating hearts and minds with its infectious music, compelling dramas, and captivating culture. From the pulsating beats of K-pop to the mesmerising performances of K-dramas, the Hallyu Experience offers travellers a glimpse into the dynamic and ever-evolving landscape of Korean entertainment.

As you delve into the Hallyu Experience, one of the first stops on your itinerary is likely to be Seoul, the bustling capital city that serves as the epicentre of Korea's entertainment industry. Here, you'll find an array of iconic landmarks and attractions that pay homage to the world of Hallyu, from the vibrant streets of Gangnam, where K-pop music videos are filmed, to the trendy shops and cafes of Hongdae, where aspiring artists showcase their talents.

No exploration of the Hallyu Experience would be complete without immersing yourself in the electrifying world of K-pop. Seoul is home to numerous entertainment agencies, where you can catch a glimpse of the rigorous training and rehearsals that go into producing the next generation of K-pop idols. You can also visit K-pop themed cafes, dance studios, and merchandise shops, where fans gather to celebrate their favourite artists and immerse themselves in the culture.

But the Hallyu Experience extends far beyond the confines of Seoul, encompassing a wide range of activities and attractions across the country. In Busan, you can visit the Gamcheon Culture Village, a vibrant neighbourhood known for its colourful murals and street art, or explore the bustling markets and seafood stalls of Jagalchi Fish Market, a favourite haunt of locals and tourists alike.

For those seeking a deeper understanding of Korean culture and history, a visit to Gyeongju, the ancient capital of the Silla Dynasty, is a must. Here, you can explore historic sites such as Bulguksa Temple and the Seokguram Grotto, which are not only UNESCO World Heritage Sites but also popular filming locations for historical K-dramas.

Whether you're a die-hard fan of K-pop, a casual viewer of K-dramas, or simply curious to learn more about Korean culture, the Hallyu Experience offers something for everyone. So, pack your bags, prepare to be entertained, and get ready to dive headfirst into the fascinating world of Hallyu – where the music is infectious, the dramas are captivating, and the memories are unforgettable.

Korean Demilitarized Zone: Border of Intrigue

Step into a realm where the past meets the present, and tensions simmer just below the surface – welcome to the Korean Demilitarized Zone (DMZ). This enigmatic stretch of land, spanning approximately 250 kilometers across the Korean Peninsula, serves as a stark reminder of the division that has defined Korea for over seven decades.

As you approach the DMZ, the atmosphere becomes palpably tense, as if the air itself is charged with the weight of history and geopolitics. Stretching from the Yellow Sea in the west to the East Sea in the east, the DMZ is a buffer zone that separates North and South Korea, marking the ceasefire line established at the end of the Korean War in 1953.

One of the most iconic features of the DMZ is the Joint Security Area (JSA), also known as Panmunjom, where North and South Korean soldiers stand face to face, mere meters apart. Here, visitors can witness firsthand the eerie spectacle of military tension, as soldiers from both sides maintain a vigilant watch over the border, ready to spring into action at a moment's notice.

But the DMZ is more than just a military zone – it's also a place of natural beauty and ecological significance. Despite its name, the DMZ has become a haven for wildlife, with dense forests, pristine wetlands, and diverse ecosystems flourishing amidst the barbed wire and guard posts. The DMZ is home to a wide range of plant and animal species, including endangered species such as the Korean crested ibis and the Amur leopard, making it a unique and precious sanctuary for biodiversity.

For those seeking a deeper understanding of the DMZ's historical and geopolitical significance, a visit to the DMZ Peace and Security Exhibition Hall offers insight into the complex history of the Korean Peninsula and the ongoing efforts to achieve peace and reconciliation. Visitors can learn about the events leading up to the division of Korea, the devastating impact of the Korean War, and the challenges and opportunities facing the region today.

Whether you're drawn to the DMZ by a sense of curiosity, a desire for adventure, or a quest for understanding, one thing is certain – a visit to the Korean Demilitarized Zone promises to be an unforgettable journey through the heart of Korea's past, present, and future, where the echoes of history reverberate and the promise of peace hangs in the balance.

Boseong Tea Plantations: Sip of Tranquility

Nestled amidst the rolling hills of Boseong County in South Korea lies a picturesque landscape that seems straight out of a painting – the Boseong Tea Plantations. Known for producing some of the finest green tea in the country, these terraced fields offer visitors a tranquil retreat from the hustle and bustle of modern life.

As you journey through the lush countryside of Boseong, you'll be greeted by the sight of verdant hillsides covered in neatly trimmed rows of tea bushes. The vibrant green hues of the tea leaves stand in stark contrast to the azure sky above, creating a scene of serene beauty that's sure to leave a lasting impression.

The history of tea cultivation in Boseong dates back over a thousand years, to the days of the Silla Dynasty, when Buddhist monks first brought tea seeds from China and began planting them in the fertile soils of the region. Since then, tea cultivation has become an integral part of Boseong's cultural heritage, with generations of farmers passing down their knowledge and expertise from one to the next.

One of the highlights of any visit to the Boseong Tea Plantations is the chance to take a leisurely stroll through the fields, breathing in the crisp mountain air and soaking in the tranquil atmosphere. As you wander along the narrow pathways that wind their way through the terraced hillsides, you'll be treated to breathtaking views of the surrounding countryside, with the tea bushes stretching out as far as the eye can see.

But the experience of visiting the Boseong Tea Plantations isn't just about admiring the scenery – it's also about immersing yourself in the rich traditions and rituals of tea culture. At the Boseong Tea Museum, visitors can learn about the history of tea cultivation in Korea, as well as the art of tea-making and the health benefits of green tea.

For those looking to indulge their taste buds, a visit to one of the local tea houses offers the perfect opportunity to sample a variety of teas, from delicate green teas to robust black teas, all freshly brewed from the leaves grown right here in Boseong. Whether you're a tea connoisseur or simply someone who enjoys a good cuppa, the Boseong Tea Plantations offer a sip of tranquility amidst the beauty of nature – a refreshing respite for the mind, body, and soul.

Daejeon: Science City Marvels

Nestled in the heart of South Korea, between the bustling metropolises of Seoul and Busan, lies a city that pulsates with innovation and discovery – Daejeon, the Science City. Renowned for its cutting-edge research institutions, world-class universities, and vibrant technological infrastructure, Daejeon stands as a beacon of progress and advancement in the fields of science, technology, and education.

As you venture into the streets of Daejeon, you'll be struck by the city's modern skyline, dotted with sleek skyscrapers and state-of-the-art research facilities. But beyond its impressive architecture, Daejeon is a city that thrives on knowledge and exploration, offering visitors a glimpse into the forefront of scientific innovation.

At the heart of Daejeon's scientific community lies the Daedeok Science Town, a sprawling complex of research institutes, laboratories, and technology parks that serve as the epicentre of Korea's scientific research and development. Here, you'll find institutions such as the Korea Advanced Institute of Science and Technology (KAIST) and the Korea Research Institute of Standards and Science (KRISS), where scientists and engineers work tirelessly to push the boundaries of human knowledge and ingenuity.

But Daejeon's appeal goes beyond its scientific credentials – the city is also home to a wealth of cultural and recreational attractions that offer something for everyone. From the serene beauty of Yuseong Hot Springs to the vibrant energy of Dunsan Dong, Daejeon offers a diverse range of experiences that cater to all tastes and interests.

For those with a passion for learning, a visit to the National Science Museum offers the perfect opportunity to explore the wonders of the natural world, with interactive exhibits and hands-on activities that bring science to life in captivating ways. Meanwhile, the Expo Science Park offers a glimpse into the future of technology, with displays of cutting-edge innovations and inventions that promise to shape the world of tomorrow.

But perhaps the most enchanting aspect of Daejeon is its sense of possibility and potential – here, in the Science City, anything seems possible, and the boundaries of what we know are constantly being pushed and expanded. Whether you're a scientist, a student, or simply a curious traveller, Daejeon invites you to embark on a journey of discovery and exploration, where the marvels of science and technology await at every turn.

Korean War Memorial: Tribute to Valor

As you step into the solemn grounds of the Korean War Memorial in Seoul, you're immediately struck by the sense of reverence that permeates the air. This sprawling complex stands as a poignant tribute to the countless lives lost and the immense sacrifices made during one of the most tumultuous chapters in Korean history – the Korean War.

The memorial serves as a stark reminder of the devastating impact of war, with its somber monuments and poignant exhibits offering a window into the harrowing experiences of those who fought and died in the conflict. Walking through the memorial's halls, visitors are transported back in time to the chaos and turmoil of the Korean War, with vivid displays recounting the battles, the hardships, and the acts of heroism that defined the era.

One of the most striking features of the Korean War Memorial is the Wall of Remembrance, a towering structure adorned with the names of over 100,000 soldiers who gave their lives in defense of their country. As you gaze upon the names etched into the stone, you can't help but feel a profound sense of gratitude and respect for the bravery and sacrifice of those who made the ultimate sacrifice.

But the memorial is not just a place of mourning – it's also a testament to the resilience and determination of the Korean people in the face of adversity. The centerpiece of the memorial is the Statue of Brothers, which depicts two brothers – one from North Korea, one from South Korea – locked in a desperate embrace, symbolizing the tragic division of a once-unified nation.

Surrounding the statue are a series of exhibits and galleries that provide a comprehensive overview of the Korean War, from its origins and causes to its lasting impact on Korean society and culture. Through interactive displays, multimedia presentations, and personal testimonies, visitors gain a deeper understanding of the complexities of the conflict and the enduring legacy it has left on the Korean Peninsula.

But perhaps the most powerful aspect of the Korean War Memorial is its ability to inspire reflection and contemplation. As you wander through the tranquil gardens and quiet courtyards of the memorial, you can't help but feel a sense of reverence for the lives lost and the lessons learned during this turbulent period in Korean history. And as you pay your respects to the fallen, you're reminded of the importance of peace, reconciliation, and remembrance in a world scarred by conflict and division.

Jinhae Cherry Blossom Festival: Pink Petal Extravaganza

Every spring, as winter's icy grip loosens and nature awakens from its slumber, South Korea's landscape is transformed into a riot of color and beauty – and nowhere is this more evident than at the Jinhae Cherry Blossom Festival. This annual celebration of nature's ephemeral beauty draws visitors from far and wide to witness the spectacle of millions of cherry blossoms in full bloom, painting the town of Jinhae in shades of pink and white.

Situated on the southern coast of South Korea, Jinhae is renowned for its stunning cherry blossom-lined streets, which come alive each April with the delicate blooms of the beloved sakura trees. As you wander through the streets of Jinhae during the festival, you'll be enveloped in a sea of pink petals, with the fragrant scent of cherry blossoms filling the air and the gentle hum of excited chatter all around.

One of the highlights of the Jinhae Cherry Blossom Festival is the Yeojwacheon Stream, a picturesque waterway that runs through the heart of the town. Here, visitors can stroll along the tree-lined banks of the stream, admiring the breathtaking sight of cherry blossoms reflected in the crystal-clear waters below. The scene is nothing short of magical, with the delicate pink petals creating a canopy of color overhead and casting a rosy hue over the entire landscape.

But the festival is not just about admiring the cherry blossoms – it's also a time for celebration and camaraderie. Throughout the festival, visitors can enjoy a wide range of cultural performances, traditional music, and dance shows, showcasing the rich heritage and traditions of the region. Food stalls line the streets, offering a tantalizing array of local delicacies and street food favorites, while vendors sell souvenirs and handicrafts inspired by the cherry blossoms.

For those seeking a more immersive experience, the festival also offers a variety of activities and events, including guided tours of the cherry blossom hotspots, photography workshops, and even cherry blossom-themed cruises along the coastline. Whether you're a nature lover, a cultural enthusiast, or simply someone who appreciates the beauty of springtime blooms, the Jinhae Cherry Blossom Festival promises an unforgettable experience that's sure to leave you enchanted and inspired.

Jjimjilbang Experience: Relaxation Ritual

Imagine a world where time slows down, stress melts away, and relaxation reigns supreme – welcome to the world of the Jjimjilbang, South Korea's beloved bathhouse and relaxation sanctuary. Stepping into a Jjimjilbang is like entering a haven of tranquility and rejuvenation, where weary travellers and locals alike come to unwind, recharge, and indulge in the age-old tradition of communal bathing.

Located in nearly every neighbourhood across South Korea, Jjimjilbangs are a quintessential part of Korean culture, offering a unique and immersive spa experience that's unlike anything else in the world. From the moment you step through the doors of a Jjimjilbang, you're enveloped in a world of warmth and serenity, with soothing music, soft lighting, and the gentle aroma of herbal remedies filling the air.

The heart of any Jjimjilbang is its bathing area, where guests can soak away their cares in a variety of hot tubs, steam rooms, and sauna chambers. From the scalding heat of the traditional hanjeungmak sauna to the invigorating chill of the ice room, there's a bathing experience to suit every preference and palate. And for those feeling adventurous, there are even specialty baths infused with everything from green tea and red wine to medicinal herbs and minerals, each offering unique health benefits and therapeutic properties.

But the Jjimjilbang experience is about more than just bathing – it's also a social affair, where friends and family gather to relax, catch up, and enjoy each other's company. In addition to the bathing area, most Jjimjilbangs also feature communal lounges, relaxation rooms, and even sleeping areas where guests can kick back and unwind together. It's not uncommon to see groups of friends chatting and laughing as they move from one spa treatment to the next, or families lounging together in their matching Jjimjilbang uniforms, sharing snacks and stories late into the night.

For those seeking a more indulgent experience, many Jjimjilbangs also offer a range of spa treatments and beauty services, including massages, facials, and body scrubs, all performed by skilled therapists using natural ingredients and age-old techniques. Whether you're in need of a deep tissue massage to ease tense muscles or a rejuvenating facial to restore your skin's glow, the expert staff at a Jjimjilbang have you covered.

But perhaps the most memorable aspect of the Jjimjilbang experience is the sense of camaraderie and community that permeates the atmosphere. In a world that often feels fast-paced and disconnected, the Jjimjilbang offers a rare opportunity to slow down, connect with others, and nourish both body and soul in the company of like-minded individuals. So whether you're a weary traveller in need of rest and relaxation or a local looking for a break from the daily grind, a visit to a Jjimjilbang promises to be a truly unforgettable experience – a relaxation ritual that's sure to leave you feeling refreshed, revitalized, and ready to take on the world anew.

Sokcho: Gateway to Seoraksan

Nestled on the picturesque eastern coast of South Korea lies the charming coastal town of Sokcho, a hidden gem that serves as the gateway to one of the country's most breathtaking natural wonders – Seoraksan National Park. With its stunning coastline, pristine beaches, and lush mountain scenery, Sokcho is a paradise for nature lovers and outdoor enthusiasts alike, offering a wealth of opportunities for adventure and exploration.

As you approach Sokcho, you're immediately struck by the town's serene beauty, with its tranquil harbor and rugged coastline stretching out before you. But it's not just the scenery that makes Sokcho special – it's also the sense of history and tradition that permeates the air, from the quaint fishing villages that dot the shoreline to the ancient temples and shrines that are scattered throughout the surrounding countryside.

One of the main draws of Sokcho is its proximity to Seoraksan National Park, a UNESCO Biosphere Reserve and one of Korea's most iconic natural landmarks. Covering an area of over 400 square kilometers, Seoraksan is home to some of the country's most spectacular mountain scenery, including towering granite peaks, cascading waterfalls, and lush forests teeming with wildlife.

For outdoor enthusiasts, Sokcho offers a wide range of activities to suit every taste and skill level. Hiking is a popular pastime here, with a network of well-marked trails leading visitors through the park's rugged terrain to some of its most scenic viewpoints and attractions. Whether you're tackling the challenging ascent to Daecheongbong Peak, the highest peak in the Taebaek Mountain range, or simply taking a leisurely stroll along one of the park's picturesque valleys, you're sure to be rewarded with breathtaking vistas and unforgettable experiences.

But Sokcho isn't just a destination for nature lovers – it's also a foodie paradise, with a vibrant culinary scene that reflects the town's coastal location and rich cultural heritage. From fresh seafood caught daily by local fishermen to hearty mountain fare served up in cozy taverns and restaurants, Sokcho offers a tantalizing array of dining options to satisfy every palate.

After a day of exploration and adventure, there's no better way to unwind than by soaking in one of Sokcho's famous hot springs, where you can relax and rejuvenate your body and soul in the healing waters. Whether you're soaking in a traditional outdoor bath overlooking the sea or indulging in a luxurious spa treatment at one of the town's upscale resorts, a visit to Sokcho's hot springs is the perfect way to end a day of adventure and exploration.

In Sokcho, the beauty of nature, the warmth of the local hospitality, and the richness of the cultural heritage combine to create an unforgettable travel experience that's sure to leave you enchanted and inspired. Whether you're seeking outdoor adventure, cultural immersion, or simply a peaceful retreat from the hustle and bustle of daily life, Sokcho offers something for everyone – a gateway to the wonders of Seoraksan and beyond.

Taebaeksan Snow Festival: Frosty Fiesta

In the heart of winter, when South Korea is blanketed in a shimmering coat of snow, the sleepy town of Taebaek bursts into life with the vibrant energy of the Taebaeksan Snow Festival. This annual celebration of all things frosty is a frosty fiesta like no other, drawing visitors from far and wide to revel in the beauty and wonder of winter.

Nestled at the foot of the majestic Taebaeksan Mountain, Taebaek is transformed into a winter wonderland during the festival, with its streets adorned with elaborate ice sculptures, snow sculptures, and twinkling lights that cast a magical glow over the town. From towering ice palaces to intricate snow sculptures depicting scenes from Korean folklore and history, the festival's displays are a testament to the skill and creativity of the local artists who bring them to life.

But the Taebaeksan Snow Festival is not just about admiring the sculptures – it's also a time for fun, laughter, and plenty of outdoor activities. Visitors can lace up their skates and glide across the festival's ice skating rink, or hop on a sled and zoom down the festival's snowy slopes, shrieking with delight as they go. For those feeling adventurous, there are even opportunities for snowboarding, snow tubing, and other winter sports, ensuring that there's never a dull moment at the festival.

Of course, no winter festival would be complete without plenty of delicious food to keep you warm and satisfied, and the Taebaeksan Snow Festival delivers on that front as well. From piping hot bowls of spicy tteokbokki and steaming cups of sweet hot chocolate to freshly grilled skewers of marinated meat and crispy fried dumplings, there's a tantalizing array of street food stalls and vendors serving up mouth-watering treats to tempt your taste buds.

As night falls, the festival takes on a whole new atmosphere, with the town coming alive with music, dance, and entertainment. Visitors can warm up by the fire pits scattered throughout the festival grounds, enjoying live performances by local musicians and dancers, or gather around to watch the dazzling fireworks display that lights up the night sky in a kaleidoscope of colours.

But perhaps the most magical moment of all comes when the festival's grand finale takes place – the lighting of the giant snow lanterns that illuminate the town square in a soft, ethereal glow. As you stand amidst the twinkling lights and falling snow, surrounded by the laughter and chatter of fellow festival-goers, you can't help but feel a sense of wonder and awe at the beauty and magic of winter.

The Taebaeksan Snow Festival is a celebration of the season's beauty and the spirit of community, bringing together people of all ages and backgrounds to revel in the joy of winter. Whether you're a snow enthusiast, a culture seeker, or simply someone who loves to have fun, the festival promises an unforgettable experience that's sure to leave you with memories to cherish for a lifetime.

Cheonggyecheon Stream: Urban Oasis

Amidst the hustle and bustle of Seoul's vibrant cityscape lies a tranquil oasis, a hidden gem that offers respite from the urban chaos – the Cheonggyecheon Stream. Flowing through the heart of the city, this urban waterway is a testament to Seoul's commitment to preserving nature and enhancing the quality of life for its residents and visitors alike.

Once a neglected watercourse buried beneath layers of concrete and asphalt, the Cheonggyecheon Stream underwent a remarkable transformation in the early 2000s, when it was restored to its former glory as part of a major urban renewal project. Today, the stream meanders for over 10 kilometers through the heart of downtown Seoul, lined with walking paths, lush greenery, and tranquil resting spots that beckon weary city dwellers to pause and unwind.

As you stroll along the banks of the Cheonggyecheon Stream, you're immediately struck by the sense of serenity that pervades the atmosphere. Towering skyscrapers give way to leafy trees and bamboo groves, while the gentle murmur of flowing water provides a soothing soundtrack to your journey. The air is clean and fresh, scented with the fragrance of wildflowers and the earthy aroma of the surrounding vegetation.

But the Cheonggyecheon Stream is more than just a pretty waterway – it's also a living testament to Seoul's rich history and cultural heritage. Along its banks, you'll find a series of beautifully landscaped parks, plazas, and public art installations that pay homage to the city's past and present. From traditional Korean pavilions and sculptures to modern architectural marvels and interactive exhibits, there's something to capture the imagination of visitors of all ages and interests.

One of the highlights of the Cheonggyecheon Stream is its impressive array of bridges, each one a unique architectural masterpiece that offers stunning views of the surrounding landscape. From the iconic Moonlight Rainbow Fountain Bridge, adorned with thousands of LED lights that dance and shimmer in the night sky, to the graceful curves of the Gwangtonggyo Bridge, there's no shortage of photo-worthy moments to be had as you explore the stream's bridges.

But perhaps the most magical time to visit the Cheonggyecheon Stream is in the evening, when the sun dips below the horizon and the stream is bathed in the warm glow of streetlights and lanterns. As darkness falls, the stream takes on a whole new atmosphere, with the sound of rushing water mingling with the soft chatter of pedestrians and the occasional notes of music from nearby buskers. It's a time when the city slows down, and the beauty of the Cheonggyecheon Stream truly shines.

Whether you're looking for a peaceful retreat from the chaos of city life, a scenic spot for a leisurely stroll, or simply a place to connect with nature and history, the Cheonggyecheon Stream offers all this and more. So next time you find yourself in Seoul, be sure to take some time to explore this urban oasis – you won't be disappointed.

Jeonju Bibimbap: Culinary Heritage

In the heart of South Korea's culinary landscape lies a dish that embodies the essence of Korean cuisine – Jeonju Bibimbap. Renowned for its vibrant colours, bold flavours, and cultural significance, this iconic dish has captured the hearts and palates of food enthusiasts around the world, making Jeonju a must-visit destination for anyone seeking an authentic taste of Korean culinary heritage.

Nestled in the fertile fields of Jeollabuk-do province, the historic city of Jeonju is widely regarded as the birthplace of Bibimbap, and it's here that you'll find some of the finest examples of this beloved dish. But what exactly is Bibimbap? At its simplest, Bibimbap translates to "mixed rice" – a hearty bowl of steamed rice topped with an array of colourful vegetables, marinated meats, and a dollop of spicy gochujang sauce, all mixed together to create a harmonious blend of flavours and textures.

But what sets Jeonju Bibimbap apart from the rest is its meticulous preparation and attention to detail. From the selection of the freshest seasonal ingredients to the careful arrangement of each component in the bowl, every step of the process is imbued with a sense of pride and tradition that has been passed down through generations of Jeonju chefs.

One of the key elements that sets Jeonju Bibimbap apart is its use of locally sourced ingredients, many of which are grown right in the surrounding countryside. From the crisp, crunchy vegetables harvested from nearby farms to the succulent, tender meats sourced from local butchers, every bite of Jeonju Bibimbap is a celebration of the region's rich agricultural bounty.

But it's not just the ingredients that make Jeonju Bibimbap special – it's also the way it's served. In Jeonju, Bibimbap is traditionally presented in a shallow stone bowl known as a dolsot, which has been heated to a sizzling hot temperature before the rice and toppings are added. This not only ensures that the rice develops a deliciously crispy crust on the bottom, but it also helps to keep the dish piping hot throughout the meal.

Of course, no bowl of Jeonju Bibimbap would be complete without a generous drizzle of gochujang sauce – a spicy, tangy condiment made from fermented red chili peppers, garlic, and other seasonings. The gochujang adds a depth of flavour and a touch of heat to the dish, tying all the elements together into a harmonious and satisfying whole.

But perhaps the most remarkable thing about Jeonju Bibimbap is its ability to transcend mere food and become a symbol of Korean culture and identity. From its humble origins as a simple peasant dish to its current status as a beloved national treasure, Bibimbap serves as a testament to the resilience, creativity, and ingenuity of the Korean people.

So if you find yourself in Jeonju, be sure to sample a bowl of this culinary masterpiece for yourself – it's an experience you won't soon forget. And as you savour each mouthful of Jeonju Bibimbap, take a moment to appreciate the rich history and cultural heritage that have made this dish a true culinary icon of South Korea.

Gyeongju Bulguksa Temple: Spiritual Haven

Nestled among the rolling hills and lush forests of Gyeongju, the ancient capital of the Silla Kingdom, lies the serene and majestic Bulguksa Temple. Steeped in history and surrounded by natural beauty, this UNESCO World Heritage site is not only a testament to the enduring legacy of Korean Buddhism but also a spiritual haven for visitors seeking solace and contemplation amidst the hustle and bustle of modern life.

As you approach the temple grounds, you're immediately struck by the sense of tranquility that pervades the air. The gentle rustle of leaves in the breeze, the soft chanting of monks in prayer, and the faint scent of incense wafting on the wind all combine to create a atmosphere of peace and serenity that is both palpable and profound.

Originally constructed in the 8th century during the reign of King Gyeongdeok of Silla, Bulguksa Temple has undergone numerous renovations and restorations over the centuries, yet its essence remains unchanged. With its graceful pagodas, intricate carvings, and ornate architecture, the temple complex is a masterpiece of Buddhist art and craftsmanship, reflecting the rich cultural heritage of the Silla Dynasty.

One of the most striking features of Bulguksa Temple is its two stone staircases, known as Cheongungyo and Baegungyo, which lead up to the main hall. Carved with intricate motifs and adorned with mythical creatures, these staircases are said to represent the path to enlightenment, with each step bringing the visitor closer to spiritual awakening.

Inside the temple complex, visitors will find a series of beautifully decorated halls, pavilions, and shrines, each dedicated to a different aspect of Buddhist worship. From the imposing Daeungjeon Hall, which houses a majestic statue of Buddha, to the delicate Seokgatap Pagoda, with its intricate stone carvings depicting scenes from Buddhist scripture, there's no shortage of awe-inspiring sights to behold.

But perhaps the most sacred spot of all is the Dabotap Pagoda, a towering stone structure that stands as a symbol of enlightenment and spiritual enlightenment. Believed to have been built to enshrine relics of the Buddha, the Dabotap Pagoda is a testament to the devotion and reverence of the Silla people, who sought to create a place of worship that would stand for eternity.

As you wander through the temple grounds, you can't help but feel a sense of reverence and awe at the sheer beauty and grandeur of Bulguksa Temple. Whether you're a devout Buddhist seeking enlightenment or simply a curious traveller interested in Korean history and culture, a visit to this spiritual haven is sure to leave a lasting impression on your heart and soul.

Incheon: Gateway to the World

Nestled on the western coast of South Korea, Incheon stands as a dynamic gateway to the world, blending modernity with a rich historical tapestry. As the country's third-largest city and home to one of Asia's busiest ports, Incheon boasts a vibrant atmosphere infused with a sense of international connectivity and cultural diversity.

Stepping into Incheon, you're immediately greeted by the hustle and bustle of a city in constant motion. Towering skyscrapers pierce the sky, their gleaming facades a testament to the city's economic prowess and cosmopolitan spirit. Yet amid the urban landscape, traces of Incheon's storied past are still visible, from the preserved colonial-era buildings in Chinatown to the ancient temples tucked away in quiet corners.

Incheon's strategic location has long made it a hub of trade and commerce, serving as a gateway for goods and people traveling to and from Korea. Its modern port, Incheon Port, is a bustling nexus of activity, handling a significant portion of the country's maritime trade and welcoming ships from around the globe. From here, ferries whisk passengers across the Yellow Sea to the nearby islands, while cargo ships ply the waters, laden with goods bound for distant shores.

But Incheon's connections extend far beyond its shores. Incheon International Airport, one of the busiest airports in the world, serves as a vital gateway for international travel, connecting South Korea to destinations across the globe. With state-of-the-art facilities, award-winning architecture, and a wide range of amenities, the airport embodies Incheon's commitment to hospitality and efficiency, welcoming millions of visitors each year with open arms.

Beyond its role as a transportation hub, Incheon is also a cultural melting pot, home to a diverse array of communities from around the world. Nowhere is this more evident than in its bustling Chinatown, where the sights, sounds, and smells of traditional Chinese culture blend seamlessly with the vibrancy of Korean urban life. Here, you can sample authentic Chinese cuisine, browse through traditional markets, or simply soak in the atmosphere of this vibrant neighbourhood.

Incheon's international outlook is further reflected in its modern skyline, where sleek office towers stand side by side with luxury hotels, shopping malls, and entertainment complexes. Yet amid the urban sprawl, pockets of natural beauty still thrive, from the tranquil shores of Songdo Central Park to the rugged cliffs of Eurwangni Beach, offering residents and visitors alike a welcome respite from the hustle and bustle of city life.

As you explore the streets of Incheon, you'll find that the city's true charm lies in its ability to seamlessly blend the old with the new, the traditional with the modern. Whether you're wandering through historic temples, sampling street food in bustling markets, or simply taking in the sights and sounds of this vibrant metropolis, one thing is clear – Incheon truly is a gateway to the world, inviting you to discover the best that South Korea has to offer.

Afterword

As our journey through the vibrant tapestry of South Korea draws to a close, it's time to reflect on the myriad experiences, sights, and sensations we've encountered along the way. From the bustling streets of Seoul to the tranquil shores of Jeju Island, each destination has offered its own unique glimpse into the rich tapestry of Korean culture and history.

Throughout our travels, we've been captivated by the warmth and hospitality of the Korean people, whose genuine kindness and generosity have left an indelible mark on our hearts. Whether sharing a meal with a local family, exploring ancient temples with a knowledgeable guide, or simply exchanging smiles and greetings with strangers on the street, we've been welcomed into the fold with open arms, treated not as tourists, but as honoured guests.

But beyond the warm embrace of its people, South Korea's beauty lies in its diversity – a kaleidoscope of landscapes, traditions, and experiences waiting to be discovered. From the soaring peaks of Seoraksan National Park to the tranquil waters of Haeundae Beach, from the bustling markets of Busan to the serene temples of Gyeongju, each destination offers its own unique blend of history, culture, and natural beauty, inviting us to explore, discover, and immerse ourselves in the wonders of this fascinating land.

As we bid farewell to South Korea, let us carry with us the memories of our journey – the laughter of new friends, the taste of delicious cuisine, the awe-inspiring beauty of ancient monuments, and the sense of wonder that comes from exploring a land steeped in history and tradition. And as we return home, may we remember that our travels are not simply about seeing new places, but about opening our hearts and minds to the world, forging connections, and creating memories that will last a lifetime.

So here's to South Korea – a land of endless possibilities, where every corner holds a new adventure and every moment is filled with wonder. Until we meet again, may your travels be filled with joy, discovery, and the spirit of adventure. Safe travels, and may your journey be as enriching and fulfilling as the one we've shared together.

Printed in Great Britain
by Amazon